Growing Up with Zara!

Authored by **Gail Ellis Brown**

Illustrated by **Ray E. Brown III**

PAGE PUBLISHING, INC.
Conneaut Lake, PA

First originally published by Page Publishing 2020

ISBN 978-1-6624-1093-2 (pbk)
ISBN 978-1-6624-1095-6 (hc)
ISBN 978-1-6624-1094-9 (digital)

Printed in the United States of America

In loving memory of my parents, Randolph and Hattie Ellis, who because of their beliefs in higher education, enabled their nine children to become successful in their chosen career endeavors.

Acknowledgment

I would like to express heartfelt appreciation to my husband Ray; daughter, Jenae, son, Ray, III, and especially to Zara, my loving granddaughter!

My name is Zara!

I am five years old!

I live with my mommy!

Her name is Jenae!

We have a dog!

His name is Caesar!

Mommy and me!

We do so many things together!

We cook our food together!

We take Caesar to the park

together!

We ride in our car; on the bus, the trains,

and ships to many places!

We even fly on airplanes together!

We have so much fun going places together!

Our dog Caesar

Caesar likes to run!

We run and play together!

Caesar likes to eat too!

Caesar protects us!

He is a good dog!

That's Me

My first cruise!

I rode a big, big ship!

It was so big!

I went far away!

I was on the Atlantic Ocean!

I saw other big ships!

I went to beautiful islands!

Things we do at our home!

I love my house!

This is our home!

We plant flowers!

I like to play in the dirt!

Planting flowers is one way I get to

    play in the dirt!

I like to watch the plants grow!

I water the plants, and the sun helps too!

When we see weeds and

    reeds in our yard, we cut the grass!

We even see snakes!

My mom is afraid of snakes!

I am a ballerina!

I spin around and around!

Can you?

I can tap dance too!

Toe, heel, heel, toe!

Tap, tap, tap!

Purrr! I'm a cat!

Just kidding!

I like cat videos!

Cats are so funny!

Do you like cats?

Do you have a cat?

I like my dog Caesar best!

I am an artist too!

Sometimes I color!

Sometimes I paint!

Sometimes I draw!

Sometimes I glue and paste to make pictures!

Sometimes I make pictures on the computer!

I make pictures on the pavement too!

I am a Girl Scout!

I love being a Girl Scout!

I have friends in my troop!

We learn different things, take

trips, and have fun together!

I have a badge for camping!

I have a badge for selling many cookies!

My vest is filled with badges I earned.

This is what I know!

I love my mommy!

I love Caesar!

I love my teacher!

I love my family and friends!

I love to dance and go places!

I love my life!

I am so, so happy!

Repetitive Words and Spelling Words

A	Our	Glue	Take	Other	Friend(s)
I	The	Draw	Have	Paste	Cook(ies)
To	Too	Just	Purr	House	Flowers
Us	Dog	Like(s)	What	Grass	Protect(s)
Is	And	Play	Five	Being	Island(s)
We	See	That(s)	Year(s)	Badge(s)	Picture(s)
My	Eat	With	Food	Scout	Family
In	Run	Love	Have	Ocean	Friend(s)
Of	Cut	Even	Much	Start	Teacher
Me	Mom(my)	Yard	Heel	Dance	Growing
Am	Fun	Dirt	Know	Plant(ing)	Selling
An	Her	Camp	Name	Watch	Camping
At	His	Grow	Park	Artist	Airplane(s)
Up	Own	Help(s)	Grass	Color	Together

Repetitive Words and Spelling Words

He	One	Rode	Reeds	Paint	Computer
So	Way	Ship(s)	Weeds	Happy	Beautiful
On	Saw	Spin	First	Funny	Sometime(s)
	Far	Each	Fill(ed)	Afraid	Pavement
	Yes	Away	Learn	Cruise	Atlantic
	Art	Went	Earn(ed)	Snake(s)	Iguana
	Are	Girl		Places	
	Cat(s)	This		Thing(s)	
	Bus	Make			
	Toe	Just			
	Can	Vest			
	You	Cook			
	Tap	Many			
	Toe	Best			
	Let(s)	Trip(s)			

Remarks!

Thank you for purchasing, "Growing Up With Zara"! I hope you enjoyed meeting Zara and her family! This publication was an introduction to Zara and what involves her present life. The forthcoming books will inspire and entertain young people who are facing comparable plights, and who are seeking explanations and solutions to everyday life encounters and dilemmas.

More adventures with Zara coming soon!

About the Illustrator

Ray has a bachelor's of arts and science degree in computer science from Georgia State University.

He is currently a senior software engineer in a large nationwide corporation.

He is also a successful music producer and artist.

About the Author

Gail has an ED.S (education specialist in administration and supervision) from Lincoln Memorial University in Harrogate, Tennessee. She also has a special education certification in learning disabilities from the University of West Georgia, Carrollton, Georgia. Gail has a master's of social service from Bryn Mawr College in Bryn Mawr, Pennsylvania. Her bachelor of science degree is from Tuskegee University in Tuskegee, Alabama.

She is currently certified as a K-12 interrelated special education teacher, school social worker K-12, and as a reading specialist K-12. Gail has received numerous professional licenses and certifications throughout her career including clinical social work in Philadelphia, Pennsylvania.

Her books are designed to encourage, engage, excite, motivate, and prepare children to be creative and successful in their future endeavors.